AF608937

For my dear parents Margarete and Jürgen and
my siblings, Gunver and Stephan

Dr. Richard Werringloer

The Little Kite Flyer

How to teach our children the art of "flying"

inspired by
Prof. Dr. Nossrat Peseschkian
Dr. Nawid Peseschkian

Drawings by

Maike Löffelhardt-Michel

1. Edition 2015

First published:
"Der kleine Drachenflieger"

Author: Dr. Richard Werringloer
Drawings: Maike Löffelhardt-Michel
Cover Design: tao.de
Layout: Lavinia Kamphausen
Translated by: Annabelle Mayntz
Edited by: Viviane Korn and Robert Gibson

Printed in Germany

tao.de in J. Kamphausen Mediengruppe GmbH, Bielefeld,
www.tao.de, eMail: info@tao.de

Bibliographic information published by the Deutsche Nationalbibliothek The German National Library lists this publication in the Deutsche Nationalbibliografie; detailed bibliographic data are available under the following internet address: http://dnb.d-nb.de.

Paperback: 978-3-95802-524-0
Hardcover: 978-3-95802-525-7
e-Book: 978-3-95802-526-4

Your children are not your children.
They are the sons and daughters of Life's longing for itself.
They come through you but not from you,
And though they are with you yet they belong not to you.
You may give them your love but not your thoughts,
For they have their own thoughts.
You may house their bodies but not their souls,
For their souls dwell in the house of tomorrow, which you cannot visit, not even in your dreams.
You may strive to be like them, but seek not to make them like you.
For life goes not backward nor tarries with yesterday.
You are the bows from which your children as living arrows are sent forth.
The archer sees the mark upon the path of the infinite,
and He bends you with His might that His arrows may go swift and far.
Let your bending in the archer's hand be for gladness;
For even as He loves the arrow that flies, so He loves also the bow that is stable.

Found in Khalil Gibran, The Prophet

Content

Preface I

Self-confident, clever children who occupy themselves and find their own way, who are joyful and attentive – who doesn't wish for this? Children need freedom, but also consistent rules, order and a clear direction in order to develop. How can we bring up our children to be well-adjusted individuals, citizens and residents of planet Earth, particularly taking into account their physical, social and spiritual basis? Bringing up children in today's world is *a heroic endeavor, almost an art*. But what is the right measure? When is it too much and when is it too little?

The following book gives systematic and practical guidance in learning and mastering this art. *The Little Kite Flyer* gives wonderfully positive insights into child development as well as into the realm of children's dreams. At the center is a holistic view of humans and their various developmental stages. The book spins a thrilling tale that parents and children can read aloud and from which much can be learned. The author's enduring and convincing expertise and his sensitivity in his treatment of parents and children is clearly apparent and is framed successfully by beautiful illustrations.

My father, Professor Nossrat Peseschkian, founder of the field of Positive Psychotherapy in which many of his works are grounded, considered work with young people and parents of particular importance. His work was influenced by the fundamental principle of the positive conception of man, namely, that people are, by nature, good.

"Consider people to be a treasure trove, rich in precious stones of priceless value. Only education can bring these treasures to light and enable humanity to derive use from it." (Nossrat Peseschkian)

My father's positive, life-affirming, well-meaning and appreciative philosophy can be sensed and felt, dear parents, throughout this successful work by Richard Werringloer. It does me good to read it and it will do you good too!
Nossrat Peseschkian has earned the merit of re-establishing the position of legends and wise tales – not only those of the Orient – as sources of healing power within the ranking of therapeutic approaches. Fables, sayings and wise tales act as mirrors of insight. Through them light can be shed on spiritual situations without the need for lengthy explanations.
It was my privilege to get to know Dr. Richard Werringloer during his training under Nossrat Peseschkian in the Wiesbaden Further Education circle and during the Bad Nauheim Psychotherapy days. In the meantime, he has not only become a very successful doctor who works with the many-faceted possibilities of my father's Positive Psycho-

therapy, but also a psychotherapist who, in the field of Positive Psychotherapy, works worldwide as an international trainer. It pleases me that we are also good friends who work together on many activities in the spirit of unity. Currently we are dedicating ourselves in Ethiopia to establishing a psychotherapeutic provision in the country following the principles of Positive Psychotherapy.

I am sure that you, dear reader, will discover many truly useful stimuli for relating to your children so that you can accompany their development in love and competence.

Nawid Peseschkian, Wiesbaden, September 2013

Preface II

Parents today are faced with great challenges arising from the process of helping children grow up. Are we up to these challenges? The Positive and Transcultural Psychotherapy founded by Nossrat Peseschkian offers valuable insight into the process of child development. For the process of growing up to be successfully accomplished there are a few important prerequisites: harmony within family and society; the utilization of available talents and resources that accompany the developmental process; transcultural encounters with fellow human beings, and true values such as love, justice, loyalty, obedience, trust and honesty, values which are not just hollow words but which can genuinely be put into practice.

As I began to read the book by Dr Werringloer, I was reminded of our family life, my own children's childhood and how we in our family experienced the three Interaction Stages: attachment, differentiation and detachment in the sense of a unity. Through the story in this book, parents and children can find a new form of relating to each other.

"If you are planning for a year, sow a seed. If you are planning for a decade, plant a tree. If you are planning for a century, then educate a person."
(Unknown source)

Manije Peseschkian/The Prof. Peseschkian Foundation

Wiesbaden, October 2013

Introduction

Positive Psychotherapy is a true-to-life method. It uses stories and wisdoms as an original transcultural approach to stimulate different forms of imagination in the framework of a resource-oriented approach. Here, we find many core messages we can take to heart.

Life is a beautiful *game* played in harmony with the laws of nature and the universe, and it astonishes and delights us every day. It is shaped *in a common effort* by many free spirits, living in the sea, in the air, in the woods, mountains and meadows. They change our world into an exquisite and sensuous pageant of colors, sounds, shapes, smells and tastes we can enjoy every day. There are countless possibilities for every living being to take part in this glass bead game, as described by Hermann Hesse. Every human being has the opportunity to consciously contribute his or her innate or acquired talents and to live expressively. A successful and creative communal game requires sincerity and respect for each of the other living beings because the rules and instruments are as diverse as this symphony's participants and as the art they create.

Only in the harmonious balance of all components can such a diverse and multi-facetted tapestry emerge for all to share and experience.
Because times, environments and societal customs are in permanent flux and constantly presenting new challenges to every free spirit, they need a high rate of flexibility and adaptability not only to manage the ever-changing circumstances, but to make the best out of them. It is equally important to have perseverance and stability to be able to develop innate abilities. To raise our children to be happy, respectful free spirits we have to be like gardeners with their flowers, laying down a fertile foundation for growth and providing the necessary stability while allowing them the freedom to develop on their own. Then it is possible for them to grow strong and reach their full height, bringing all their abilities and potentials to fruition.
You can use this book in many different ways. It is particularly suited to be read aloud, or browsed through together for inspiration. Taken together with its reflective comments, it forms a common foundation for exchange and discussions, questions and answers, and invites you to reflect about your own wishes, dreams and fears. It is a compact handbook on education, with the main emphasis lying on freedom and joy.
But above all, dear reader, do discover in these pages a message of the beauty of this process of self-development, and nurture your inner joy to unfold. Discover the magnetic power of collaborative creation.

Chapter 1

The festival

Once upon a time, in a country beyond your dreams, and at a time even your grandparents cannot remember, there lived a couple of artistic kite-flyers together with their son. Their names were Volavento and Regina and their little son was called Peppino. They served at the court of the mighty King Massimo as conductors of the Royal Kite Air Force, which entertained the court on special holidays with aerobatics. On such a holiday, it was the harvest festival, the powerful ruler and his beautiful wife, his glorious knights and the entire people gathered on the hill in front of the castle gates. Everyone wanted to enjoy the great spectacle which was about to happen high up in the air. It was a beautiful summer afternoon, the sun had already passed its peak and a warm breeze wafted in from far-off regions of the land. It brought scents of foreign spices, landscapes and cities with it. The people gathered on the festival grounds were all dressed in their finest fancy garb frolicking around the colorful stalls which had been especially set up for this event. Games, food and drink for the pleasure of everyone were offered. All around one could hear the laughter and bustle of the cheerful crowd.

As the time of the flight performance drew near, it suddenly became silent on the meadow and among the stands. Everyone sat down and expectantly looked up into the sky, waiting for the annual performance to begin. Then, suddenly, there they were. From high above the clouds, as if conjured into existence, the kite flyers appeared in a dense rain of confetti. They rushed daringly towards the crowds, hanging from their daredevil kites, turning agile loops – alone, in pairs or in threes – and barely cleared the heads of the spectators. They painted colorful circles and shapes in the afternoon sky and their wings made wonderful whistling sounds that sometimes even sounded like the melody of a song. The crowd sat there, their eyes and mouths wide open in amazement. Some adults almost fell backwards off their chairs – as they used to do in school in the old days. As the kite flyers finished their artistic demonstration, they flew one last elongated arc and landed in front of the king and queen. They bowed and thanked their monarchs while the court cheered with enthusiasm and one could hear repeated shouts of "Encore, Encore, Encore," from the crowd, which means something like "one more time" in noble circles.

Peppino was giddy with excitement and as always particularly proud of his parents, who, in his eyes, were the greatest and most daring among the aerialists. Impatiently, he waited for them to finally end their conversation with the king and to come to him. At last, Volavento turned around to his young son laughing, lifted him in the air and hugged him tightly to his chest. Peppino shouted with glee, overjoyed to have such a strong father with such zest for life – a father who loved him, one he could have daily adventures with and who would tell him new and exciting stories from the great wide world. His mother Regina came running as well, gathering into her loving arms the son who was always playing tricks on her and making her laugh. Volavento had met her on one of his many world travels. She was a very gifted kite-flyer and defeated him in one of the major aerobatic tournaments, something he did not like to admit. It was during that time they discovered their love for one another, and together they competed in and won numerous competitions. Out of sheer joy over their newfound happiness and with their spirits full of adventure, off they flew to discover the remotest corners of the earth. They saw countless new and amazing things and had great and exciting adventures.

On this festive day Peppino was extremely excited. As Regina and Volavento let go of him and Peppino faced them, he suddenly said: "I want to be a kite flyer just like you two!" He had long felt that flying was the most beautiful thing in the world to him. To float high in the air, then swoop down to earth, again and again, doing spins and loops. He had even been daydreaming about it, sitting on a bale of hay on a balmy summer day, watching the birds fly by. But Peppino also understood that it would not be easy to learn the art of kite flying. He knew it would take hard work and a lot of effort to wrest the wind's secrets from it and to practice and internalize aerobatics step by step. His father had told him again and again how often he had been standing on a hilltop, alone or together with others, to practice safe starts, gliding and landing. How often had he fallen, getting bruises, even breaking a finger before he mastered safe flying! The true art of flying, not only simply gliding up and down, he did not learn until much later, through experience. He always called it "the feeling of becoming a part of the wind and air" and talked about the experience of "becoming one with the elements".

It was on one of his discovery flights through distant countries that he met a wise old flight instructor who was to stay in his memory his whole life as a person and as a flying artist. Never had he seen such great pleasure and enthusiasm for flying and never again would he learn so much from a single teacher. It was he who helped him to feel the wind, to glide like a proud eagle and to become the happy person he was today.

Volavento was happily surprised and beamed at his son, saying: "Wonderful, there is no better present you could have given us! I have always hoped you would become a little adventurer someday." He took a deep breath, seated himself on a tree stump in the midst of the meadow and sat Peppino on his knee: "Now we have to plan how you can rise up in the air and fly away soon." Volavento's expression turned thoughtful. Regina joined the two and said: "Marvelous, that is just wonderful. But tell me, Peppino, why do you want to become a kite flyer?" The boy looked at her wide-eyed: "Why?" He had never asked himself that question, although the answer seemed clear to him. He had always felt a longing to explore the world and discover its secrets. And after all, he wanted to glide through the air like his parents did. When Regina looked at her Peppino daydreaming she whispered: "Why don't you tell me what you see." And all the fantasies and wishes he had about kite flying came tumbling out of his mouth. His parents were glad and hugged their Peppino tightly to their breast. Volavento said enthusiastically: "Exactly how it happened to me." The three of them liked to be together, they felt content and secure in their little family.

After this exciting afternoon they were all hungry. They stood up, took each other by the hand and strolled towards their home, following the path down the hill. Together they prepared a festive dinner, and Volavento and Regina regaled Peppino with stories of the adventures and escapades of their youth.

Positive conception of man and the world, or: The development of a creative self-image

For our children to have a happy childhood and adolescence and for them to become mature, creative and energetic adults, it is necessary that they perceive their environment as comprehensible. They need to have the feeling that their actions can induce change, so that they can find meaning in the occurrences around them over the course of their development. When they receive the necessary attention and affection, together with stimulating challenges, they can embark bravely on a journey of discovery and realize their own potential. But if their experiences are to the contrary, they will feel irritated, hurt and defenseless, and develop a feeling of privation and worthlessness.

To become strong and healthy adults our children need to develop a positive conception of humanity and the world through good role models. This worldview is the source each child can draw upon for creativity, energy and initiative. Without good role models the path of development becomes harder and longer. It might even lead to seemingly insurmountable difficulties and disturbances while discovering one's own abilities and during the later detachment from the parents. A positive conception of humanity and the world is not only important for children, but for every person regardless of age. In this day and age of multi-layered challenges and crises, which we extract from the permanent stream of impressions from the media landscape, it is not easy to create and maintain a positive conception of humanity and the world. Having a positive outlook on life does not mean to go through life with rose-colored glasses downplaying or suppressing hunger, conflicts, or environmental catastrophes. Nor does it mean to only acknowledge and glorify the beautiful and pleasant sides of daily life, which of course exist in abundance. It rather implies that we acknowledge the existence of both phenomena and their complex entanglement. It is good to realize that it is possible for us to be happy in this complex world and that we can enrich it with our own and collective existence.

In Latin, "*positum*" means the "given", the "provided". This means there are many more aspects to be valued than we would have thought at first sight. Our brains, specialized by evolution for problem–solving, first perceive the challenges any situation presents us with, in the service of protection, safety and stability, before allowing us to recognize the beautiful sides we could just as easily turn to. How else could we have faced the dangers of prehistoric times? But how we consciously deal with the "provided" is primarily our own decision. Which perspectives would we like to open up for ourselves?

We are born into this world and can as equally search for meaning in it as give it meaning. Every profession, every hobby, every little thing we do – making music, painting, cooking, sewing, gardening, communicating, driving a car or even just brushing our teeth – means that we are playing, musically, upon the laws of the universe, mingling with its harmonies and creating our own pieces. Even dissonances are harmonies as we know today. A Tibetan Buddhist proverb says: "*Every word is wisdom purely because it exists.*" Herein lies the admiration for everything that exists as such, for nature with all its variety of colors, sounds, senses, tastes and everything else. Every being plays with the laws of nature in its own way and combines them in new compositions of color, shape and sound. These merge to a new overall picture of nature, constantly varying its beauty with the passing weather and seasons. Every weather, every season has its own mood and its own special character. When we are quiet we can recognize and appreciate it.

In a brief moment, opening our eyes consciously, we can reawaken our curiosity. If we hit "pause" in our otherwise so fast-paced life, in which we are mostly just rushing from task to task, we can manage to reacquire the openness of our children for the abundance of beauty in all of nature. This reminds us of the words of Jesus in Matthew 19, 10-13: "You shall become like children for theirs is the kingdom of God."

It is possible to change our life, which often has become a perpetual cycle of habits, into an upwardly moving spiral, restoring its purpose and direction. Do we want to realize – you and I– that we have the chance, in this world of laws and harmonies which we've inhabited since birth, to actively build on and transform the joy and beauty of the world through our own personal contribution, which we received from nature, the universe, or God?

Hinduism has the saying: "Atman seeks to express Brahman," which means something like *The single soul tries to manifest the world soul.*

"Man is a mine full of precious gems that are only waiting to be discovered and polished." This Bahá'í proverb expresses all the meaning of life and the full joy of discovery, which is borne together by so many people of different religions and ideologies. Let us all, together with our children, enhance the diversity and beauty of the world and work creatively on our common future.

The Date-Eater

A woman came with her little boy to the wise Ali and said: "My son is suffering from a serious problem. He eats dates from morning till night. If I don't give him any dates, he screams his head off. What shall I do? Please help me. " The wise Ali looked at the child kindly and said: "My good woman, go home and come back at the same time tomorrow." The next day, the woman and her son again stood before Ali. The great master sat the boy on his lap, spoke to him in a friendly way and finally took the dates out of his hand and said: "My son, think always of moderation. There are other things that taste good." With these words, he let the mother and child go. The woman, who was somewhat puzzled, asked: "Great master, why didn't you say that yesterday? Why did we have to make the long trip to you a second time?" "My good lady," Ali answered, "yesterday I couldn't have convincingly told your son what I told him today, because yesterday I myself had savored the sweetness of the dates."

(The Merchant and the parrot)

"The job of the educator can be likened to that of a gardener who tends different plants. One plant loves the blazing sunshine, the other loves the cool shade; one loves the riverbank, the other loves the barren mountain top. One prospers best on sandy ground, the other on soft clay. Each must receive the appropriate cultivation; otherwise the result will be unsatisfactory."

Abdu'l-Baha

Conception of man in Positive Psychotherapy

In every human being lies the ability to grow in love and knowledge.

*Generally, people do everything to the best of their abilities.

*Everything a person does serves a purpose or has a good reason and can be a foundation for change and development.

*Every human being has the need for love, respect, understanding and security, even if he or she cannot show that due to inner trauma.

*Every form of acting out is an attempt to protect oneself against a perceived threat.

*Healing is a process every person has to go through for themselves, yet others can lend their support.

*Change and growth are ongoing processes; nobody can nor has to do everything in one day.

*Whatever happens in a family system is the product of each member's contribution. There is never only one person responsible for the result of a family. This is why we should change the question "Whose fault is it?" to "How can each member of the family assume responsibility for what happens?"

Chapter 2

Peppino's first kite

The next morning Volavento and Peppino got up at the break of dawn and left the courtyard in the first golden rays of sunshine and walked passed the pine tree grove to the hangar. This was where the kite collection of the parents was carefully stored and lovingly maintained. All the kites were ready to go at all times and safe to fly. Peppino was so excited he had barely slept all night, tossing and turning and dreaming of the most daring stunts. But eventually he did get tired and fell asleep. Before long, though, the roosters started crowing, and he could hear the floorboards creak as his father came to wake him. His first flying lesson was waiting for him. "What, you're still asleep in bed?" Volavento cried out when he opened the door and looked into the dusky room. "Are your kite flying dreams so beautiful that you don't want to wake up? Rise and shine! Today we start to make your biggest dreams come true! Remember, it is not enough to only dream your dreams, one has to tackle them to make them come alive." Peppino looked at his wise father with big eyes and was suddenly wide awake. He jumped out of bed and sprang into his clothes so that he could get down to action with Volavento.

Peppino had seen the kites many times. But today they seemed to have a special shine and extra magic. Now he saw the many different shapes, colors and sizes of the kites, which his father had all built himself, through different eyes and asked himself: Why all this variety? Would one good kite not be enough? Almost as if he had read his thoughts Volavento said: "As you can see, there are many different kinds of kites which can be used for flying special and sophisticated kinds of stunts. They are painted in different colors to bring joy and delight to the spectators at each performance. However, the shape and color of a kite are not the most important features. You will have to be sure that your first kite flies steadily, otherwise the first downdraft or a single wrong move will make you fall from the sky. Once you have mastered the art of safe flying, you can make improvements to it and fiddle with its details. Let your imagination run wild and beautify it any way you like. But now it is time to start! We want to build you your own unique kite, completely tailored to you and your needs and wishes."

Volavento scratched his stubbly chin with a serious expression: "You will also have to complete a lengthy lesson-plan, for flying has to be studied and practiced! It is the same as with the kite itself: it is a symbol and a key to becoming a successful kite flyer. You will see." With these words Volavento pulled a beautiful multicolored kite off a rack suspended from the hangar's ceiling. "Do you see this quadrangle in the form of a diamond? This shape represents the foundation for a safe flying machine. It is designed to human proportions and is, therefore, exceptionally easy to steer in the air. This diamond will also remind you of the four areas body, work, friendship and vision of the future. These four aspects are what life comes down to. If you want to lead a happy and fulfilled life as an artistic kite flyer, then always remember this and try to keep the four aspects in balance. They will also help you to be successful in competitions because they will provide you with strength, stability and peace of mind."

Volavento now pointed to the top end of the kite and explained: "This first corner shall remind you of the reason for being a kite flyer. It should always challenge you to find new goals in life and to think about what life means to you and what you want to achieve in it and beyond. I want to give this advice to you, my son, so it can accompany you on your life's journey: Always remember that man is a mine full of precious gems and that everyone has the ability to bring her or his own sparkling treasures to light, as to bring joy to others and themselves."

Volavento pointed out through the gate into the wide open world and attuned Peppino to the abundance of colors and shapes, spread out right before their eyes. At the same time he put a hand behind his ear and bade the astonished boy to listen for all the voices of the animals and the wind. "The world is like a glass bead game," he said, "a unique work of art, consisting of the most various laws which make themselves perceptible as shapes, colors, sounds, tastes and many things more. We cannot recognize everything at once. The wise man I told you many stories about when you were younger once told me that we humans are the eyes of this beautiful nature, of the entire universe, eyes through which it can recognize itself. And if we want to really, truly live, we can play on the keyboard of nature's laws, which we also know as harmonies. If we do that our life becomes art and gives pleasure to us and everyone else. There are different ways to reach this playing stage. For example, we can elevate flying to an art form, a chef prepares the most delicious meals, a gardener creates a colorful garden, a musician plays beautiful music or a farmer tills the land... there are many more examples, but I think you know what I mean." Peppino slowly and thoughtfully looked up at his father. "Do you mean I could transform my whole life, every single day and deed into an 'art'?" he asked. "I think that is exactly what the old man had achieved and what he talked to me about," Volavento answered, and in that moment he himself understood this wonderful truth properly for the first time.

The two of them walked back to the middle of the hangar, to the space with all the different kites. "This second corner here will remind you of your physical health. Without it you will never completely master flying." Peppino tugged at his father's sleeve. "Do you remember the musketeers? To become good fencers, they had to practice jumping, turning, running and lots of other things as well," Peppino added before he did a cartwheel and almost crashed into a kite leaning against the wall. "Oh yes," his father laughed heartily, "that is precisely what will have to improve a bit. But there is still plenty of time for that. I will show you appropriate exercises later, and also talk to you about a proper diet and the necessary breaks. And don't forget, in doing so, you will cut a fine figure for the girls as well" Volavento said smiling, while Peppino looked sheepishly into a corner. He had tried time and again to impress a girl he secretly had a crush on with particularly artistic gymnastic exercises, and it happened regularly that he crashed through a window or into the pond again; one time he even plowed into his teacher's nose. His father of course had caught wind of these heroics. "Now for the third corner, which stands for your profession, should you decide to stay a kite flyer. Make sure that your work truly brings you joy; above all else, aim for that. Learn to read the signs in the air that warn you of the downdrafts and updrafts and how to spot a thunderstorm closing in. There are other things that are equally important for successful kite flying, like knowing where you want to go, constant practice and wholehearted commitment. But your friends and family also play an important part. They can offer support and advice when you need it. It is important to have a few good friends, in good times as in bad. People you can do things together with and who help set your mind on a new path are worth their weight in gold. This is what the fourth corner should remind you of." Volavento tapped the corner of the kite with his index finger, producing a gentle, thumping sound.

Peppino was overwhelmed by all these words. His head was literally spinning. He would never have thought that there were so many rules to learn and obey to become a really good kite flyer. But now it was time to build his own kite. First, Volavento took Peppino's measurements. After that he explained the basic guidelines for building a kite, especially how he could make his kite easily steerable. He also showed Peppino how to saw, plane, bend and glue the wood to acheive the necessary flexibility, strength and lightness. Father and son worked together for almost an entire week. Every day Peppino had to demonstrate his patience and perseverance at work and make sure that every detail was taken care of. When he went home in the evenings he was tired but very satisfied. Finally, on the sixth day, the time had come. There it was, in the middle of all the wood shavings: the new kite, his kite. The sailcloth covering its frame was radiant, still all white and empty. Now the final thing for the young student to do was to choose a nice picture to paint on his kite. He had thought long and hard and came up with so many ideas that he had trouble choosing one out of all of them. In the end, he decided on a proud falcon against a deep-blue sky. Exhausted, and with this picture in his mind, he went to bed and dreamed that his falcon would carry him out into the wide world.

Four modes of life, or: The discovery and development of personal talents

If we give our children a framework for their joy of discovery, providing a comprehensible and malleable environment they can directly interact with – according to Aaron Antonowsky, Sociology professor and discoverer of salutogenesis – then they have the possibility to discover their environment with joy and curiosity and thereby participate in the eternal *game of the universe*. They will start searching for their own talents and realize them. Our little discoverers should be introduced to the world in a varied and age-appropriate way, without demanding too much of them.

At every age our children develop special abilities to absorb impressions and to collect experiences. As an infant they will start their journey of discovery by experiencing their surrounddings suckling and touching. Everything is taken into the mouth and examined. Over the next months, hand and arm movements are coordinated more easily, and they watch their hand movements with great fascination and a bit later the playful interactions these hands can create with their environment. Proportionately, in keeping with the increase of mobility through crawling, and later through walking and running, the experiential horizons of our growing children also expand.

Of course, we as their parents and the rest of their immediately accessible surroundings are in the center of their lives and interests in the beginning. Every mother has an especially close contact to her baby through breastfeeding in the first months. But the father too should seize the opportunity to feel the closeness, to marvel at the almost magical development of his child and to witness and support the constant expansion of its experiential field. Through playful interaction and in caring for his child he can provide a soothing closeness and warmth.

Our little free spirits experience and observe their own needs attentively, the way they make themselves known and the way their environment reacts and tends to them. Experiences are collected and added to their personal treasure trove of experiences, to be drawn upon and modified in later encounters. Every child collects immediate experiences in their family of origin, later in their expanded environments in four categories, further described in the following. These experiences lead to the development of the media of the capacity to love, which lead to the formation of all interpersonal relationships within and outside the family.

In this way, we the parents and the environment influencing our children contribute a formative influence on the capacity for contact and attachment, interaction and differentiation, as well as on all the processes of detachment. These, alongside the genetic factors, significantly determine how a person will interact with groups and what qualities these contacts will demonstrate. Every child experiences, on the one hand, their own value through the parents' affection and the interaction with their person, later called "I". On the other hand, it experiences through the relationship between the parents, namely, how they care for each other and which rules exist in their life together, the relationship modes which will greatly influence the child's own behavior patterns in two-person relationships and especially in interactions with the "You". In addition, the child observes, as mobility and perception increase, the parents' relationship to their social environment, their relationship to a "We", and with awakening intellect also the parent's relationship to world view and religion, the so-called "Primal We", which lays an important foundation for the development of one's sense of security.

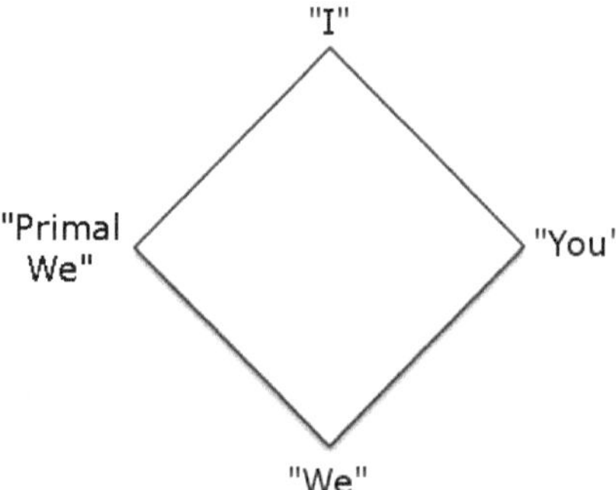

Fig. 1: The four model dimensions in the development of the capacity to love

In these four categories, defined in *Positive Psychotherapy* as *I, You, We* and *Primal-We*, the child collects experiences that will

influence its own self-image and self-confidence in the future. The openness and capacity to act spontaneously are also dependent on the variety and type of success they've experienced.
In the child's continuing development, both education and transfer of knowledge play two important roles: the basic capacities of each and every human being to learn and to utilize experiences for a benefit. The vehicles for this capacity to know are the body with all its senses to perceive the environment, the mind which processes all these impressions, and tradition, which enables the passing on of knowledge from generation to generation. Furthermore, there is intuition, creatively achieving new insights from things known and surmised. The coordination of more or less all of these instruments is decisively influenced by our subconscious.

All the experiences a child makes from the beginning of its existence influence its perceptions, feelings, expectations, attitudes and its way of thinking. They also determine the individual sphere of education and learning through the linkage with the capacity to love.

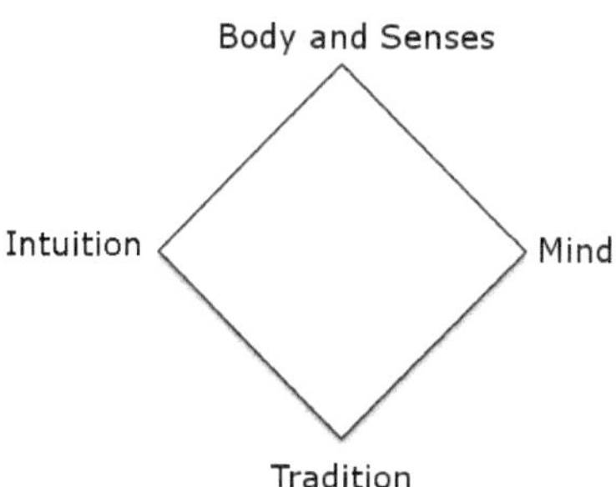

Fig. 2: Four dimensions for the development of the capacity to know

The child learns to develop its own personal consciousness of its body in the course of growing up. It discovers what it can achieve with its body and which capacities it can develop. Moreover, in the process, it perceives the boundaries it encounters. It discovers a complete range of movements, different foods, ways to dress and groom oneself, and experiences many little adventures which occasionally might involve injury or pain. You could say that the child learns about its body's parameters. The child experiences different levels of joy and satisfaction, e.g. while running, doing somersaults, enjoying its favorite food or in the way it dresses. All of these experiences are connected to its own *body*. In preschool or kindergarten, later of course in school, the child discovers many more ways to use its intellect and capacity to learn in order to discover the world. It has now reached the life stage of *achievement*. The child has reached a differentiated understanding of its environment and is capable of using every newly acquired ability to better control and influence its environment. This way, the child acquires more and more self-determination and self-confidence. In dealing with other children and adults it experiences an expanded social acknowledgement through the different forms of contact, interaction, experience with emotion and conflict with others. In the course of childhood and adolescence new fantasies about the future take shape, as do concepts for the immediate or longer-term future, and also an idea about the meaning of life – our own or in general, the before and after, and what it means to be human here on this earth.

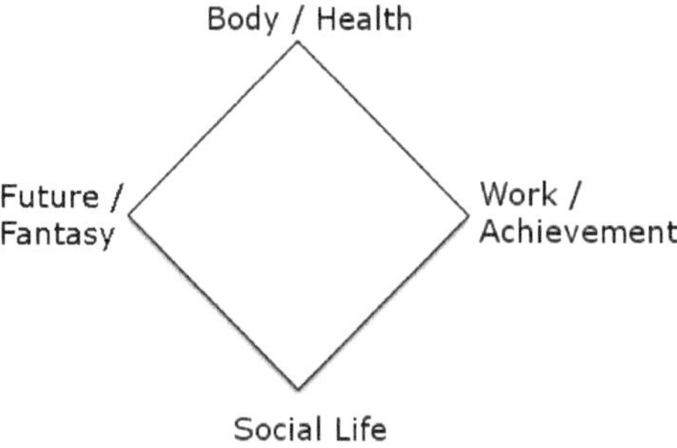

Fig. 3: Four modes of life

Summarizing, one can say that our own experiences as well as the ones made around us are absorbed and adapted by our children like water by a dried-out sponge. Later in life these experiences form our children's inner world and determine their cognitive and behavioral capacities. Therefore, it is vitally important to offer them a wide field of experiences in which we can actively support them as they discover their own abilities.

By the time our children reach adulthood we want them to be independent in all four areas of life, to have developed individual cognitive, emotional and physical abilities which allow them to take care of their health, work for their livelihood, be socially integrated and have a meaningful and creative self-image and world view. A person who is comfortable in his or her own healthy body, who has a profession he or she enjoys, and financial stability, who is embraced in a harmonious circle of friends and family and has a life-affirming philosophy or religion is equipped with all the necessary components to lead a happy and fulfilled life and to meet with confidence any challenge the future may hold.

The important qualities of the four areas of life are, firstly, the *body* comfortable in itself and its *health*, maintained by a positive self-image, physical activity, hygiene, a healthy diet, good sleep and a satisfactory sex life. Secondly, we need to learn and to practice a meaningful *profession* which corresponds to our abilities and preferences and which provides a pleasant working atmosphere, manageable yet stimulating challenges, and a salary that secures a good standard of living. Furthermore, it is important to have a fulfilling *social life* with good and stable friendships and family relationships and the time to enjoy them as well. Last but not least *fantasy* and *future* play a meaningful part, characterized by the care and development of a positive world view, an individual religion or life philosophy and by taking the time for creative hobbies and shaping the future.

There will always be problems in every life: with your health or your work, in your social life or in your faith. But if you are securely rooted in your four areas of life and manage to keep them in balance, you will be much more able to brave life's storms and to maintain your happiness and positivity than someone who has not developed his areas sufficiently.

A Chinese tale from Liezi

Kongzi was contemplating the waterfall of Lü Liang, which plunged thirty fathoms to the river bed and for miles caused the water to froth and churn so violently that even turtles, fish and newts could not swim in its murderous current. There he saw a man swimming down this treacherous river. Kongzi thought that this man must be embittered and seeking to end his suffering, so he sent his disciples to the river to fish the man out. The man, however, emerged from the river a few hundred paces further on, dried his hair and even sang to himself as he wandered about on the bank of the torrent.

Kongzi went to him and asked in wonder: "The waterfall of Lü Liang plunges thirty fathoms to the river bed, causing the water for miles around to froth and churn so violently that even turtles, fish and newts cannot swim in its current. As I saw you swimming there, I thought you were embittered and seeking to end your suffering. I sent my disciples to fish you out. However, you emerged from the waters, dried your hair and sang as you wandered the bank. I then thought you must be a spirit. When I look closely, though, I see you are a man. May I ask if there is some secret Dao that allows you to walk on the water?

The man spoke. "No, I harbor no secret. First I had to habituate myself, then it became my nature and is now my destiny. I let myself be drawn in by the consuming vortex, and rise up again with the frothing swirls. I follow the reason of the water, and do nothing myself. That is why I can move freely in it.

Kongzi then spoke: "What does that mean: 'First I had to habituate myself, then it became my nature and is now my destiny'?"

The man spoke to him: "I was born in these hills, and I feel at home inhabiting these hills. That is the habituation. I grew up in the water and feel at home in the water: that is my nature. Without knowing why I do this, I do it this way. That is my destiny."

(Chinese Tale)

"All children are growing
Even in the cold of winter
Growing very quietly
They get smart and wise
If you watered them
They would become giants."

Gottfried Herold

Key points for fostering children's self-confidence

The education of your child starts the day it is born – here you can lay the foundation of all education.

*The child develops best when it knows that it is the most important person in your life and is loved and respected unconditionally.

*Your praise, encouragement and the marking of recognizable progress strengthen you child's sense of self-worth.

*Your parenting should not accelerate your child's development, but utilize the child's abilities and possibilities from day one.

*Children have a great capacity for learning and need as many good opportunities as possible to experience this in a variety of ways.

*Children want to be encouraged to be active, but they do not want to be forced.

*Children want to have a big area of freedom to show their newly developed skills.

*Newly developed skills are always worth their reward.

*If children want to learn something they need you to help. Keep it to a minimum.

*Children want to have the chance to test acquired skills in every new situation.

*Children need as much contact to other people as possible.

*Children need a positive environment in order to develop and thrive in a carefree way.

*Not all children are the same; familiarize yourself with your child's individual character.

*Children need stable relationships and your presence as parents, but also your love, your understanding and your tolerance.

*You can learn to understand your child's signals.

Chapter 3

First attempts at flight

And so the day arrived for Peppino to rise up into the air for the first time, even though it would only be for a few short exciting moments. Regina absolutely wanted to be there to watch her son's first big jump. Volavento and his wife prepared to give Peppino a demonstration flight so that he could observe how it was done correctly. The three of them stood high upon a hilltop looking down into the valley carpeted with flowers. They could see their house between the neighbors' fields, meadows and farms. Taking turns, Volavento and Regina ran downhill with their kites into the wind, lifted off and, after turning a little loop, landed gently on the same spot they had lifted off from.
"It looks so easy when they do it," thought Peppino and wrinkled his forehead worriedly as he looked down into the valley. Despite all the daredevil tricks he had secretly and fearlessly performed, his tummy felt queasy and his hands were jittery. Of course his parents had explained to him how

to steer his kite and had warmly reassured him when he asked if he could really do it, and if nothing could happen to him. "Just take a look at how we do it and try to copy us. You'll quickly feel how your kite reacts and realize that the beginning is not all that hard. It's not a problem if you fall; what's important is that you always have to get up and try again. Skill comes with practice." Still, he could not shake the thought: What would happen if he crashed? In his imagination the hill became a big mountain peak and the bushes high and threatening treetops towering in his way. He saw himself hanging helplessly from one of the treetops, unable to get down. Regina took her son by the hand and said: "Listen Peppino, I will tell you a little story! Maybe it will help you to conquer your fear." She paused meaningfully and then quietly started her tale:

"Our king was once searching for a new vizier. The vizier is the most important adviser in the royal court. The king had ordered that all the wisest men of the land be called to him and put to a test so that he could find the most capable one of them all. Can you imagine? He had a colossal gate built with a heavy and devilishly complicated lock. The wise men were then commanded to approach and try to open the lock, thereby unlocking the massive gate. Faced with such a large lock, a great majority of the candidates respectfully conceded, saying: 'My word, no, I could never open that.' Some approached more closely and inspected the lock, only to back down out of fear of failure. Only one had the courage to rattle at the handle of the door and behold! The door opened by itself. It had namely not been locked at all and had only appeared to be closed. All it took was the courage to try. Naturally, the dauntless wise man won the competition and was appointed the king's vizier."

"So, my little one, now it is your turn to show how big and brave you are and that you are ready for your test," Volavento said smiling. Peppino looked at him defiantly and thought: "who are you calling 'little'?" He was still feeling a bit queasy but the story he had listened to attentively had given him courage. He grabbed his kite, ran a few steps downhill and there! ...at once he was in the air, gliding over the hillside. He laughed – everything seemed so easy now! The air tousled his hair and he felt weightless. He looked down at his parents, beaming. At that moment his kite veered sharply off to the side; by turning his head so suddenly he had shifted his weight. He saw himself closing in on a piece of turf as if in slow motion, which in a flash he grazed with the edge of his kite. Then everything went helter-skelter as he tumbled down the hill and came to rest buried underneath his kite. Volavento and Regina came running, picked up his kite and laughed out loud as they lovingly wiped the cow pat he had unfortunately landed in from his forehead. "Don't worry," his mother chuckled lovingly, "we chose this hill so nothing could happen to you". Suddenly Peppino had to laugh as well. And he understood his lesson: by crashing he had learned how to steer, the magic formula is in shifting your weight!

In the trials to follow he managed to stay in the air longer every time, and even the curves and landings became easier and softer. When on one of the next days he discovered the updraft and managed to really gain a few meters of altitude Volavento and Regina shouted: "Brilliant! This calls for a celebration!" Peppino invited all his friends to tell them about his latest great adventures.

The correct motivation, or: There's a special magic in every beginning

Children are full of love for life and full of spirit of discovery. They turn over every stone, experiment with everything they encounter outside in nature and find their personal boundaries there as well. The child thinks: "The oven is hot, I can burn my fingers. If I jump into that puddle, I will get wet and my clothes will cling to my body. Running around without a sweater in the cold of winter is uncomfortable and careless, I will get cold and even catch a cold. If I slide around on the grass or in the mud, I will get dirty."

Caution is required when the little ones are off on a new adventure in their environment. But we should not smother their amazing abilities to discover things on their own by applying too much control, help or anticipation. It is better to support them in experiencing their environment in an active but secure way. While doing so we, as adults, can rediscover old secrets we thought forever lost. We cannot expect our children to be able to do everything from the start, e.g. being "house-trained", or eating by themselves, or always be the first to learn something new and do it best. Our little free spirits do not get delivered as complete little adults to the cabbage patch. They need lots of love and patience to make every little step in their development corresponding to their age, before they can be released into the world as independent. All along the way little crises lie in wait but those can be overcome together when we are attentive and perceptive. The best way is to help our children find their own solutions to challenges. Solving them for them or even keeping all problems away from them takes away their chances to develop important abilities and skills for dealing with obstacles and hurdles on their own.

Stories, wisdoms, anecdotes and jokes can be very helpful in education. They stimulate our charges' fantasies and can offer a deeper understanding of certain situations without having to live or even suffer through it themselves. Other people's experiences are valuable, your own experiences are priceless, or so the saying goes. We can use the reflective nature of stories in a pleasant and even humorous way and thus offer a possible solution for a challenge they are currently up against. Throughout history, in many cultures and peoples, stories were told to children and parents for this purpose, passed on from generation to generation. Famous examples are the Brothers Grimm fairy tales and the Tales of 1001 nights, which also transcend their educational aspect to achieve medical-psychological value and are used by many doctors to help their patients in the face of crisis.

No Master falls from the sky

A magician was performing his art before the sultan and winning the enthusiasm of his audience. The sultan himself was filled with admiration and exclaimed, "God, help me, what a miracle, what a genie! "

But his vizier gave him pause for thought as he said: "Your highness, no master falls from the sky. The magician's art is the result of his industriousness and his practice. "

The sultan wrinkled his brow. His vizier's disagreement had spoiled his pleasure in the magic arts. "You ungrateful man" How can you claim that such a skill comes from practice? It is just as I said: either you have talent or you don't. " He looked at the vizier contemptuously and cried. "You don't have any talent anyway - away with you to the dungeon. There you can ponder my words. And so you won't be lonely, and so you will have one of your kind right there, you will have a calf as a cellmate. "

Starting on his first day in the cell, the vizier practiced picking up the calf and carrying it up the steps of the dungeon tower. Months went by. The calf grew into a powerful steer, and with each day of practice, the vizier's power increased.

One day, the sultan remembered the man in the cell. He had him brought to him. When he saw him, he was overcome with amazement. "God help me, what a miracle, what a genie. "

The vizier, carrying the steer on outstretched arms, answered with the same words as the other time: "Your highness, no master falls from the sky. In your mercy you gave me this animal. My strength is the result of my industriousness and my practice. "

(The Merchant and the parrot)

"Every child is an artist.
The problem is
how to remain an artist
once we grow up."
Pablo Picasso

Protection and benevolence for maintaining the inner balance

Give your children your trust so they can trust themselves.

*Children have the capacity to learn independently and to overcome manageable difficulties.

*Cultivate a fair and appreciative interaction within the family to create a feeling of equality and attachment of all family members.

*Stay "real" in your behavior and stay yourself, as this will help you maintain credibility and your children will turn to you in a crisis asking for help and you can stand by them.

*Be conscious parents, take on your parental role and spend time with your children.

*Allow your child to have attachment figures beside yourself.

*Provide your child with basic trust and encourage love for life and curiosity.

*Convey faith and a mental-spiritual background.

*Display an optimistic attitude towards all things.

*Create a content and happy atmosphere.

*Create emotional security and show authentic and constructive solutions in conflict situations.

*Find a good way to deal with stress for yourself and your child, a positive approach to resolving conflicts and establish the art of saying "no".

*Live rhythmically, do things slowly and take breaks. Take occasional detours.

*Be responsible for your physical health.

*Do not lose track of your own needs.

*Children and parents are allowed to make mistakes. Let go of perfectionism!

Chapter 4

Approaching thunderstorms

Many months passed and Peppino could feel himself becoming more and more secure during his flight lessons. Regina and Volavento still accompanied him to his practice flights. They had taught him a lot: different flying techniques, basic knowledge about up and downdrafts, meteorology, common air traffic laws, with right-of-airway, and flying on the right and left, as well as a little bundle of tricks he was especially proud of. One afternoon after school while his parents were still busy at home, they sent him ahead to tidy up the hangar. While he was working he discovered a new and especially striking kite. An eagle was painted on it and it looked really fast and maneuverable and it was a good size for him as well. Peppino quietly whistled to himself and thought: "Look at that, it's perfect for me! My parents will be a while, so why not try out this sleek little speedster". He quickly slipped into the harness of the kite and indeed – it fit him like a glove.

Peppino grew impatient. Where were they? He did not want to sit around all afternoon and be bored. He had even tidied up already so what was next? Then he thought he could fly a round on his own, his parents would certainly come and find him. He slipped back into the harness of the new kite and ran outside into the wind.

A hundred times Regina and Volavento had told him to look out for cirri and cumulus clouds especially, oftentimes they were forerunners of approaching thunderstorms with hail and lightning. They also brought treacherous wind shears with them and were feared on the windward side of the kingdom, where they were not uncommon. But Peppino was so busy with the new kite that he literally threw caution to the wind and completely forgot about it. Only when the clouds started to block out the sun and it got darker and darker around him and lightning flashed fierce and blinding did he realized how far he was from home and how everything on the ground had become smaller and smaller. Now woken up from his exciting game, he tried to orient himself. The castle and the town close to his home were barely visible behind the next line of hills. They did not seem as far away as he had feared earlier. His concern was a different one: he was still climbing. He had started his descent but the ground did not come any closer. Even though Peppino tried to descend in spirals the ground seemed to get further and further away from him. Oh no! He must be caught in one of these infamous updrafts other kite flyers had told him about. It could happen that these dangerous winds whirled kite flyers into the peaks of the highest clouds where they were helplessly exposed to the elements. Not only would it be incredibly stormy but also freezing cold. Suddenly, Peppino realized the danger he was in. The rumble of thunder was closer than before and the dark clouds around him were eerily lit up by lightning. The ground seemed to be further away than ever.

"What am I going to do?" he asked himself fear-struck. His home seemed to be hopelessly far away and out of reach. Now the rain and gusts of wind started. His kite was thrown back and forth; it was almost impossible to control it and his arms started aching from the effort. His situation seemed hopeless. When escape seemed impossible he saw a black dart flying towards him. It was Regina. "Thank God, here you are. We have been looking for you all over the place, how did you manage to get into this mess and how are we going to get you out again?" she called out to him with a serious face. "You have to do exactly as I do. You will have to learn your first nose dive today. Be careful that you always keep your kite steady and yet still try to preserve your strength. You will need it when we have to break all the momentum we gathered once we get close to the ground. Remember, that is the crucial moment! I will always be close." Peppino looked at her, his face ashen. He was left speechless. "Have faith!" his mother gave him a wink and turned round to nose dive. Peppino followed his mother head first towards the woods and the houses, down from dizzying heights and at breakneck speed. Soon the small dots became recognizable as rooftops. When they were even closer and Peppino started to fear that all his momentum would smash him to pieces on the ground, his mother pulled up the tip of her kite. Peppino followed her using all his strength. Suddenly, the horizon was back on eye level and mother and son zoomed along over fields and meadows and further with all the momentum they had gathered up high taking them almost right up to their doorstep.

Volavento let out a deep sigh of joy and relief when he saw them from afar, for he had been looking for them for a long time. Quickly he turned around in an elegant curve and hurried to meet the pair, who were speeding like falcons across the landscape. Just as they arrived home and had packed their kites away safely it started to rain, and Peppino started to cry. He really had been very scared and it was literally a last-minute rescue. Both parents hugged their shivering, half-frozen boy. They took him inside their warm house and the last thing he remembered before he fell into bed completely exhausted was Volavento's voice telling him: "Your first nose dive didn't look bad from far away, but next time we'll practice that calmly. By the way, the kite you took was meant to be your start-of-school present."

Crisis as a chance, or: Challenge as potential for development

One question keeps coming up again and again. Every day we observe people in our surroundings – at home, in our hometown, in the newspaper and on television – people who have to shoulder heavy burdens, those who face great misfortunes, those who have to suffer. It does not matter if it is about accidents, illnesses, loss or catastrophes; looking at these moving tragedies we keep asking ourselves: Why us, or why this or that person and why is there so much suffering in the world in general? How can the world we live in make sense, how can it be a wonderful game when there is so much unhappiness. Sometimes the world can even seem to be a kind of "hell". We long for a land where problems and suffering do not exist, we wish for a paradise where nothing bad can ever happen.

Science and rationality tell us that life without problems and tasks would be a life without progress and change, and that without suffering and the overcoming of painful situations there would be no development on our planet. Therefore, every problem already carries in it the chance for a new beginning, a developmental step on the individual and collective level. A problem or crisis might even bring us a step closer to world development. We can look at the problem as a kind of bus stop where we can get off, take a different bus and continue in another entirely new direction.

A problem is a task that we have to master but also a chance for change in our life and personal growth. Circumstances, situations, indeed the nature of things themselves call for a *direct approach* above all else. We cannot simply close our eyes or postpone them indefinitely. There is a saying that goes like this: "Who does not move with the times, will be removed over time." This happened to the dinosaurs, the mammoth and the sabre-toothed cat. This law of constant change, which requires a deep capacity to adapt, applies to all living beings, also to us humans.

We have many possibilities to influence the fate of our planet not only through our consciously lived life but also through the way we educate our children. The sentence "*The children are our future*" should inspire and challenge us because people are not happy when they do not have problems but when they know how to deal with them.

We make a fundamental distinction between two types of destiny: the *conditioned* and the *unconditioned*. Conditioned destiny is what we call everything that reacts upon our own actions. Buddhism speaks of the *Law of Cause and Effect*. That is a very theoretical way of saying something like "What goes around comes around". Or like in this Indian wisdom:

"The one taunting the tiger needs long legs". An unconditioned destiny, on the other hand, is an occurrence in our life that we cannot influence, e.g. our birth, our death, an earthquake, a flood or winning the lottery, even though it is obvious that we can influence them to some degree. The rule of conditioned destiny teaches us that we are part of our own well-being or misery. Another saying goes like this: "Every man is the architect of his own future," even though a helping hand is always appreciated.

A person going through life in a constant bad mood, insulting and attacking other people all the time, will eventually meet an equally nasty response, no matter how patient his surroundings. Another one who is convinced of his own failure in everything will have a hard time succeeding at anything, let alone find satisfaction in the appreciation if something did work out. That is what we call a *self-fulfilling prophecy*.

Actions, but also personal attitudes and conceptions, always have consequences.

Especially in education it is therefore important that we approach our children with patience and love but also with the necessary strictness. Everything we confront them with will be absorbed, processed and woven into their world view and surfaces again eventually in their behavior. One of our most important tasks as parents is to provide our children with a good tool for handling conflicts and problems. The easiest way to do so is to be a good role model.

A good model

A mullah wanted to protect his daughter from the dangers of life. When the time had come and she had grown into a flower of beauty, he took her aside and told her about the baseness and malice of the world. "My dear daughter," he said, "remember what I tell you. All men want only one thing. Men are cunning. They set traps wherever they can. You don't realize how you sink deeper and deeper into the swamp of their desires. I want to show you the way of unhappiness. First the man swoons about your best features, and he admires you. Then he invites you to go out with him. Then the two of you pass his house, and he mentions that he just want's to fetch his coat. He asks you if you wouldn't like to come in the house with him. Upstairs he invites you to have a seat, and he offers you some tea. The two of you listen to music, and when the time is right, he suddenly throws himself on you. In this way you are violated, and our good reputation is gone. "

The daughter took theses words of her father to heart. Some time later she came up to her father and smiled proudly. "Dad," she asked, „are you a prophet? How did you know how everything happens? It was just as you described it. First he admired my beauty. Then he asked me out. As if by coincidence we passed his house. There the poor fellow noticed he had forgotten his coat. And so I wouldn't be alone, he invited me to come on into his apartment. As good manners require, he offered me tea and brightened the day with beautiful music. At that point, I thought of our words and I knew exactly what would happen. But you see, I am worthy to be your daughter. When I felt the moment coming, I threw myself on him and violated him, his parents, his family, his good reputation, and his esteem! "

(The Merchant and the parrot)

"The adult values acts, the child values love."

Indian proverb

Educating is relating, or: Conversations with Children

Talk to your children properly and seriously; this teaches them to take on responsibility and comprehend the realities of life.

*Encourage your children to develop creative solutions to problems and let them help implement them.

*Speak openly about the quality of the current relationship to help make them conscious of the variety of quality in relationships.

*When they have the chance to talk about themselves, children will learn from them.

*Stay relaxed in your role as parent and always set boundaries clearly, kindly, well in advance and unequivocally.

*Practice constructive and solution-oriented criticism which doesn't fixate on the problem or come across as condescending. This helps in raising your children to be emotionally non-violent and competent.

*Don't do all the difficult things for your child. That way it can learn to solve problems on its own.

*Give your child responsibility.

*Set up clear rules and comprehensible structures and give notice of exactly what is to be done.

*Don't compare your child with other children or siblings, otherwise, it will feel manipulated.

*Always bring up positive points before negative points: first praise, then criticism. Give feedback.

*Clearly indicate what behavior you expect from your child. Prepare for resistance and don't take it personally.

*When a situation is difficult, don't let yourself lose your composure. Avoid unnecessary fussing.

*Do not publicly admonish your child, not even in critical situations.

*Correct your child only in one thing at a time.

Chapter 5

Kite flying school

The day after Peppino's dramatic excursion everyone was happy that they all made it home alive and unhurt, but there were also some warning words that needed to be said because he had brought all of them in a very dangerous situation. Since Peppino showed real remorse and was deeply troubled about the consequences of his actions, the serious talk was also forgiving and heartfelt. Regina and Volavento taught their son many more lessons about how to handle the kite in dangerous situations and showed him many more tricks to master the difficult winds of the kingdom. Never again did they have to scold him for such disobedience. The fright he had given himself was so great that he decided to wait with further excursion until his skills had improved.

During the next months, kite flying school really took off and Peppino was happy that his parents had given him such a beautiful, fast and maneuverable kite for the start of school.

He really owned a wonderful flying machine and no other kite in his class could compare in beauty and refinement. The time for his first solo flight was approaching much faster than he thought. The first days of school flew by and very soon he was allowed to fly to and from school all on his own. Of course, he had to prove that he had not only learned all the air traffic rules of kite-flying by heart, but that he could also act on them and ascend quickly should another kite flyer close in on him from the right or from below. These were the right-of-airway rules in the kingdom and if you wanted to avoid trouble you had better to stick to them.

But also insisting on one's right-of-airway could be very dangerous. His schoolmate Roberto had learned that the hard way too when he tried to enforce his right against a goose. The outcome was a crash sending both of them tumbling from the sky and Roberto head first into the chimney of the castle. He actually got stuck so tightly that it took the king's knights to end his misfortune, some pulling, some pushing him to get him out. And not to forget the beautiful princess who, sitting at the fireplace reading and having just reached the most suspenseful page of her book filled with ghost stories, genies in a bottle and magic lanterns, was so frightened by the clouds of soot and the sparks coming out of the chimney that she could not stop sneezing for three days straight. What lasted even longer than her sneezing was the people's laughter about Roberto's singed hair. None of the other kite-flying pupils wanted to share in Roberto's fate.

Peppino loved his flying lessons, even though he sometimes found it hard to sit still for such a long time every morning at his school desk and he was not so sure about the usefulness of boring subjects like calculus, reading and writing. He more greatly enjoyed the technical and practical lessons which resulted in him teetering on his chair in the more boring lessons or playing tricks on the teachers with his classmates. They kept hearing that these subjects were important later in life, but soon he realized that they came in handy for flying as well, which definitely interested him the most. They had just started to build kites with an especially broad wingspan in class. They were to be designed to cover long distances at great altitudes with a minimum of effort. Peppino was very excited. He could hardly wait to finish this new "bird" and try it out. He put his kite together piece by piece, becoming faster all the time, and in all his eagerness to finish he also became a little inattentive. He could not wait for the glue to dry or for the wooden ribs to take on their final form. Quickly, he had moved on to the next step and that's when it happened. He had overlooked a detail in the construction manual, had only looked at the drawings without properly reading the content. The kite he had built looked rather nice, and he had given special attention to the painting, but something just did not seem right. This *bird of paradise* of his looked a bit strange. When it finally had the necessary strength and Peppino wanted to try it out, he realized that he had mounted the control frame, which he was to hang from and steer the kite with, the wrong way round. The feeling of disappointment and defeat was overwhelming. What should he do now? All the hard work seemed to be for nothing.

The other pupils finished their work one after the other and immediately wanted to do a test flight with their teacher. Peppino sat there and could not even manage to loosen the harness. It was glued tight – in gluing, at least, he had done a very thorough job. "Darn it," he called out, "do I have to learn to fly my kite backwards now?" The teacher came over and could not suppress a smile when he saw Peppino with his kite and the harness the wrong way round. His classmates hooted and doubled up with laughter, and they taunted: "It really is a bird of paradise you've got there, can't find one like it in any textbook". But shortly afterwards they all helped him to repair his mistake. The teacher had promised that either all of them would lift off together, or none of them would. Peppino, with the help of his classmates, managed to rebuild his kite and thus avoided having to learn how to fly a kite backwards. Shortly before sunset all the children were ready and flew into the evening sunset.

Over the years, Peppino became a better and more respected pupil. His parents were always happy with his grades. But he was not satisfied with all of that. He became more ambitious and wanted to be the best in everything, passing all exams with flying colors. Peppino's life was suddenly filled with studying and there was nothing else that interested him anymore. He sat quietly in his room every day, studying with dogged determination. He practiced flying with equal concentration. When the time for the first big exams came closer he so completely buried himself in his school work that his parents started to have worries about his diligence. Peppino had become increasingly solemn; he did not laugh any more, and he did not even take part in the shenanigans at school anymore. He had stopped playing with his friends and riding his unicycle. He circled forlornly through the air or sat hour after hour at his desk until the letters blurred and his eyelids drooped. He became pale and tense and nervous. His friends did not know what to do with him anymore. All he could only talk about were the exams, and it was getting boring. They even started to make fun of him. "There he is, the little eager beaver, wants to be best pupil!" Peppino was getting more tired and more exhausted every day, so much so that he could not answer the easiest questions in class. Sometimes he blacked out, and his face flushed red. Regina and Volavento, who had been watching Peppino for some time with increasing worry, did not know what to do. For all their evening talks, nothing had changed. Finally, Volavento had an idea to save the day. He pulled a big, gilt-edged book off the top shelf and sat down on the big cozy carpet to read the young lad a story.

The perfect camel

Years ago, four scholars travel through the Kawir desert with a caravan. In the evening they sat together at the fire and talked about their experience. They were all filled with admiration for the camels. They were amazed by their contentment, they admired their strength and they found their modest patience to be the almost incomprehensible. "We are the masters of the pen," the one said. "Let's write or draw about this animal this way to praise and honor the camel." As he said these words, he took a roll of parchment and went into a tent that was lit by an oil lamp. After a few minutes, he came and showed his work to his three friends. He had drawn a camel just getting up from a resting position. The camel was so well drawn that one would almost think it were alive. The next man then went into a tent and soon came out. He brought a short factual depiction of the advantages that camels bring to a caravan. The third wrote an enchanting poem. Then a fourth man finally went into the tent and forbade the others to disturb him. A few hours later, the fire had gone out, and the others were already asleep. But, from the dimly lit tent, there still came the sound of the scratching of the pen and the monotonous song. The next day, the three waited just as futilely as they'd waited for their colleague on the second and third days. Like the cliffs that had closed behind Aladin, the tent hid the fourth scholar. Finally, on the fifth day, the entrance to the tent opened up, and the most industrious of the industrious stepped out, dead tired, with black-rimmed eyes and sunken cheeks. His chin was framed by a stubbly beard. With tired steps and a look on his face as if he had eaten green lemons, he approached the other men. He wearily threw a bundle of parchments onto the carpet. On the outside of the first roll he had written in large letters, "The perfect camel, or how a camel should be..."

(The Merchant and the parrot)

When Peppino heard the ending he heaved a heavy sigh. He realized he had been caught up in his ambition. *More* was not necessarily *better*. As a rule, he learned and studied much better when he was happy and well-rested. He passed the exam not quite as well as he had thought he would. But he was happy again and could celebrate passing the exam together with his friends and parents.

Over-challenged and under-challenged, or: The little kite flyer in a tailspin

For our little kite flyers it is very important to learn strategies for self-protection and self-assertion from an early age to develop the capacities for orienting themselves in their environments. To express themselves creatively they need to make developmental steps that are connected to regional and cultural circumstances. They also have to be appropriate for the child's age group.

When children grow up overly protected and spoiled, kept apart from the realities of life out of fear for their well-being or not being challenged enough, they will have trouble collecting experiences and developing routine skills to master difficult situations later in life. Even normal and age-appropriate tasks like a change of school, starting an apprenticeship, a voluntary social year or going to college can turn into unfamiliar and overly challenging situations which may trigger considerable emotional distress or even turn into a serious life crisis.

Children and young adults from an overly protected childhood can become like daisies in the wind. If they do not have the means to protect themselves and to stand firm, they will be torn back and forth by the winds of demand and – in the worst-case scenario – they will snap. To try to catch up to the age-appropriate maturity in social abilities at a later stage will require a lot more effort and cause more mental strain for the children and adolescents than the original normal conflict with their environment would have.

Thus said, an overly strict or overly challenging education can lead to significant developmental delays or even to life-long emotional and social difficulties. A child cannot develop freely in an atmosphere that is too rigid or overly protective. Later in life it will always shy away from every challenge, out of fear of failure or out of fear of punishment. The adolescent in this case can also use an escape route that is very unpleasant for the parents. It is possible that he or she will rebel during puberty and venture to escape with the same force that was used to press him or her into a box. He or she will completely withdraw from the influence of the desperate parents.

In a rigid form of education children are treated like bonsais, where the roots and shoots which they would need to develop their creative potential are cut off. The lack of *the life blood of love* and the strangulation of growth will either lead to a child growing up into a stunted plantlet or a bristly thistle. Here, *parental fears* play a leading role as they do in cases of overprotection. These fears can manifest themselves in different ways, e.g. as the fear that the child does not adhere to concepts of morality, that it will not be the best pupil, that it will not find its own way in life, but generally they become manifest in the parent's fear of their own child's independence and otherness.

In contrast to the styles of education mentioned earlier, a permissive anti-authoritarian education can lead to a child not knowing or not being able to maintain its boundaries, later leading to painful experiences with the outside world when it learns that society places a certain degree of demand on them. Looking back on all three educational styles we can conclude that a balanced accompanying of the child, consisting of freedom, support and loving guidance when necessary, is the best support while it discovers its environment.

Giving children growth support means giving them stability on their way to the light, just like when a plant climbs a trellis. When they reach puberty, adolescents practice their independence and assertiveness. Again it is important to neither smother their natural efforts nor give too much freedom. To give support as well as allow for situational resistance is most certainly not easy, but it is worthwhile cultivating this high art to allow the adolescents to *sow their wild oats* and yet encounter security on their way to maturity. Especially rebellious teenagers need a safe haven when they are struggling with feelings of shame or regret.

To provide helpful support to our young free spirits we have to offer them these three things: the necessary love to draw strength from for their own growth; the right support that lets them obtain stability; and security and a high degree of freedom to unfold their full creative potentials. If we provide that, we will never have to fear for them, even if they start going into a tailspin in one of life's storms. They will always manage to steer their kite safely back on a self-determined course.

The Owner of the Bow

A man once owned an exquisite bow made of ebony with which he could shoot very far with amazing accuracy, and which he valued above all else. One day, though, as he was inspecting it with an admiring eye, he remarked to himself: "You are a bit too homely, aren't you! Your only ornament is your sheen. What a shame!" Soon, however, he had an idea. "We can remedy that! I shall go to the best craftsman and have him carve figures into the bow." He went to the carver, who engraved his bow with a full representation of a hunt. And what better scene to have on the bow than a hunt? The man was bursting with joy and shouted: "You deserve these decorations, my dear bow!" He raised the bow, drew the string – and the bow snapped in half.

(based on a fable by Gotthold Ephraim Lessing)

"Tell me, and I will forget it.
Show me, and I may retain it.
Let me do it, and I will learn the skill."

Johann Wolfgang von Goethe

Feedback, encouragement, basis for discussion and the settlement of conflict situation

Harbor realistic expectations towards your children.

*Help your child with playing, learning, keeping discipline and in creating its environment.

*Accentuate the positive to make your child feel comfortable in its own skin and to give him or her balance.

*You should be able to recognize problems, address them and give advice.

*Take your children's feelings seriously and give feedback.

*Anticipate emotional crises and approach them together with your child instead of waiting and punishing.

*If the child utters a bad word, do not react immediately. Give yourself and your child time.

*Show your child that you have been hurt by its words, e.g. "That hurt me..." Do not judge and use I-messages.

*Establish real contact and be absolutely clear.

*Believe in, see, and talk about the good in your child.

*Try not to give a backhanded response. Taking offense and striking back do not make sense.

*The more children withdraw, the more it is your task to establish contact again. If necessary seek professional help.

Chapter 6

Flying together

The exciting exam was finally over and the young kite flyers were overjoyed to have passed. Only one of the boys, whom the others called Sleepy, had failed once more and had to repeat the year. The teachers and even his parents were already used to sending him into the same class over and over. And like after every exam for the last 33 years he said: "No matter, I'm really looking forward to the fun I'll have with my new classmates next year – and also to the pranks we're going to play on the teachers."

The holidays had arrived and with them the time for the infamous flying holiday camp. It was the summer highlight for all the children and they were very happy to go. They would sleep in tents and have barbecues. They could run wild, play with their friends and sometimes there was even a treasure hunt where everyone wanted to be the first to find the treasure. The teachers in camp had planned something really special for this year. They wanted to put on an air show with the children and have the school orchestra play music. All the kite flyers were asked to contribute their special talents and show what they could do. Everyone was allowed to give a taste of their talents and show a special trick on the first day. The boys and girls knew many different stunts and boastfully demonstrated their abilities. Some were really good with loops and twists, others incredibly fast or astonishingly slow. And they had a few nose diving artists among the young talents who had mastered the daredevil art of braking right above the spectator's heads. It was good to know that all of them had learned to look out for their own safety and that of the others. Rule number one was that the person who endangered him or herself or others was not allowed to continue to fly until he or she thought better of it and had to do some hours of community work. That could mean many weeks of mucking out the stables or cleaning the castle moat. Of course those were the most despised of the children's 'favorite' chores.

Now they all stood on the big green hill next to the castle. There, on the meadow, is where they would practice in the coming weeks for their air show. If they succeeded, it would be their first performance for a big crowd. Peppino and his friends had a funny feeling performing in front of so many people. Everyone was invited: The King and Queen, the court, all the townspeople. All of them would watch and the children were eager to give their best and show off their skills and courage.

The next morning they had try-outs and everyone was assigned a role in keeping with their abilities. The teenagers were in a cheerful mood when they talked over dinner about the challenges to come.

One scene proved to be very difficult during the training and was a challenge for the teamwork abilities of the boys. The kite flyers who were able to fly slowly and steadily were supposed to make a big circle while some of the lighter female kite flyers were supposed to come in from the outside and, with a loop-the-loop, gently land on the wings of the boys' kites. When that was accomplished, they would ascend as a double pack in a spiral while three nose divers plunged through the circle towards the spectators. Wow, what an amazing stunt that was going to be! Everyone thought that. And because everyone wanted to be the center of attention at the beginning and because it was much easier to blame someone else for a mistake, everything was an unholy chaos. Peppino was particularly good at contributing to the chaos and absolutely wanted to be first to fly through the circle to impress his sweetheart Rebecca. He managed to disturb the rhythm of the whole group with his shoving and his abrupt movements which scattered the figure. Even though all the teachers repeatedly implored him to hold back he kept barging through the group until he bumped into Olli, one of the slower kite flyers, sending Olli and Peppino's own beloved Rebecca tumbling through the air. The teachers could only shake their heads helplessly. What were they supposed to do with this little show-off? He simply would not listen to their advice and be a team player to make the figure look beautiful and harmonious. Instead he caused pandemonium day after day until, soon, everyone was spinning through the air.

After the accident, Peppino was suspended for the afternoon and had to watch while his teachers were thinking about a disciplinary measure for him. First they considered banning him from the show all together, but then they would be missing a kite flyer and such a good one at that. He would be sorely missed in the show and of course it would be decimating for him not to participate. Then they had a better idea: why not let him swap with Olli? He could take part as a slow flyer since he apparently already knew how to nose dive. This way he could learn the quality of slow flying as a "punishment". Of course he still had to clean the moat, no exceptions, even if he was a nice boy. So Peppino spent many hours of his free time with baleful chore of giving the castle moat a thorough scrubbing. Before he was allowed back into training, the group leader Alfredo wanted to recount a story to make him remember his lesson even better.

Heaven and Hell

A long time ago our ruler went to see a great prophet, for he had a question which was troubling his heart and he wanted to know if the prophet could find an answer to it. The ruler asked: "What is the difference between Heaven and Hell?" And the prophet answered: "Ah, follow me, I can surely show you." The two walked down many long corridors, deeper and deeper into the inner realms of the palace, past great halls and vaulted chambers until they came to a room redolent with the wonderful scent of a great pot of soup that steamed in its middle. The room thronged with people, rich and poor; all of them wanted to eat of the soup, but they all looked starved and emaciated. Each of them had a long metal spoon with a wooden handle in their hand which, due to the boiling soup, were very, very hot. They tried again and again to eat from the spoons, but these were so long that they couldn't bring the soup to their lips, instead spilling it on themselves or their neighbor. Their laments tore the air. The prophet turned to the ruler, gave him a long, knowing look and said: "You see? This is Hell!" The two continued through the palace, down more long hallways and corridors until they came to another room which also smelled deliciously of soup. This time, they beheld a completely different scene. Nothing but joyous, laughing people were to be found here. They were all well-fed and helped each other to eat the wonderful soup. In turn, each would carefully raise the long-handled spoon to his neighbor's mouth, so that everyone was sated and no-one was hurt. This time, the ruler look long into the eyes of the prophet and said: "So this must be Heaven?" The prophet smiled silently.

(The Merchant and the Parrot)

In the next days Peppino kept thinking about how he had made a complete fool of himself in front of Rebecca and all the others. Afterwards, he felt really embarrassed about the accident and he was happy to have been spared a more drastic punishment. This turned out to be a blessing in disguise, however, as he would now be carrying his sweetheart Rebecca. Nothing could go wrong now. He wanted to show her that she could rely on him.

They practiced for many more days in big and small groups and Peppino was particularly full of enthusiasm whenever he was able to fly with Rebecca. With every repetition the group became better attuned to one another. The time came when they practiced with music for the first time. All the movements and turns had to be carried out to the rhythm of the music. That was not at all easy, but at the same time it was a lot of fun. Keeping the rhythm was hard, and in the beginning everyone was all over the sky. But they kept on practicing and slowly their movements became harmonious and beautiful, and the kite flyers seemed to meld in wonderful interaction. Peppino felt like a sky dancer. He waltzed Rebecca elegantly through the clouds. What a heavenly delight to dance with the others and Rebecca in harmony! That Rebecca felt the same about him became clearer the more they practiced together. They liked to dance together so much that they often stayed longer to work on some figures. Sometimes his turns were too big for her or hers too fast for him. But every day they became more attuned to one another and were able to learn many tricks and secrets from each other.

Then the big day arrived and all the people of the little kingdom gathered again on the big festival grounds. There was music and fancy market stands with colorful fruit, fresh vegetables, savory cheeses and many more delicacies, which had been harvested that summer and then exquisitely prepared. For their prosperity and their community everyone wanted to give thanks to Nature and the Creator on this festive day. The people tried to outdo themselves every year with an even more beautiful festival, which somehow worked like magic. Regina and Volavento were there of course, and the parents of all the other children had long since arrived. Nobody wanted to miss the show and everyone was eager to watch the little kite flyers. Peppino's parents had given him a new costume for the occasion. He would cut a fine figure in it as he slowly sailed down over the spectators' heads. Peppino was so nervous that his forehead glistened with perspiration and in his haste he had put his shirt on inside out. If it hadn't been for Rebecca, who saw it immediately, he would have taken off like that. "Are you going to put your shirt on the right way round? Otherwise you won't only fly like a fool but look like one as well," she joked.

"Are you ready? Up, up, and away, the others are waiting for you!" Regina urged. "Break a wing," Volavento said with a big smile. "We are not going to take that literally," Rebecca replied chirpily and the two little artists vanished into the colorful kite flyer-children's-cloud.

The musicians began with a piece to put people into the right mood for the air show. The children ran off with their kites and sailed into the late summer wind. At the signal of their flight conductor they started the performance. The crowd was swaying to the music while the little aerialists presented their program whose choreography they had practiced so diligently over the last weeks. The music and the performance delighted the audience, and their "hurrahs" and "bravos" could be heard high in the sky. The youngsters could see people throwing confetti and tinsel around. When finally the kite flyers presented their most difficult figure everyone stood gazing open mouthed at the spectacle, rooted in amazement to their spots. Nobody made a sound. Only when the figure was finished did the people start breathing again, and a tidal wave of enthusiasm went through the crowd. When the performance came to an end, there was applause from everyone, and again they called "one more time" like they had done before for the adult performances. When the music sounded for the last time, the kite flyers from Regina's and Volavento's formation suddenly grabbed their kites and climbed up into the sky to dance together with the boys and girls. The orchestra had to keep playing because nobody wanted to stop dancing.

Primary and secondary capacities – 5 step confict-resolution, or: Cohabitating with other free spirits

The incredible abundance offered to us by the universe is already obvious when we take a look out of the window into our surroundings. Nature unfolds in front of our eyes as a myriad sound, shape and color composition we can enjoy over and over again. To achieve such diversity, nature's great and small things have countless properties and qualities. When we take the time to observe them attentively and in peace and thoughtfulness, we will find that every season, every climate possesses its own beauty. We can even befriend cold and rainy days while sitting at the fireplace with a cup of tea or admiring a clear blue sky above a snow-covered landscape. Special moments occur when we suddenly notice a shimmering rainbow after a thunderstorm or feel the first snowflakes of the year, which we all-too-often miss out of eagerness to be busy.

All the people inhabiting our planet appear in a great diversity. Unfortunately, we do not always manage to approach this kaleidoscope of personalities in a friendly and happy way. The incredible variety of capacities and qualities people develop, their opinions, body types and looks, origins and cultures continue to provoke prejudices fueled by inner fears. It is astonishing how fast these prejudices vanish when we overcome our inhibitions and come to know people thus seeing a totally different conception of man than we imagined before. Sadly, we experience again and again how a person, a population or a so-called race seems to some people unpleasant, abhorrent or heinous. *Someone else* will stick out by virtue of his *different* way to dress or to move, by *different* manners or a *different* language, a *different* way of being punctual, a *different* sense of personal hygiene, a *different* way of expressing hospitality. Being different, otherness, be it pedantry, lax morals, slowness, hectic behavior, an unfamiliar skin color and much else can lead to being perceived as unlikable or even threatening, simply by failing to meet a *different* person's arbitrary standards of social acceptability.

And yet it is the differences that make human life so wonderful. They are useful and necessary for the survival of the human species. They signify strength and adaptability and help humankind to survive and to develop new forms of culture. The division into positive and negative character traits mainly originates from a misunderstanding of others' qualities and from a lack of insight how useful these capacities could be for their owner, his environment and by extension maybe even for you as part of that environment. Prejudices often originate from unconscious fears of getting hurt, being placed in an uncomfortable situation or being confronted in a negative way. Every character structure shows strengths and weaknesses where its sphere of influence overlaps or does not overlap with a compatible field. The creative spirit of an artist will thrive much more in an inspired atmosphere than inside of rigid guidelines, for example, whereas the energy of a person with a love for nature might wither in a sterile surroundings, and a mathematician might need virtual fields of activity to achieve peak performance through complex thinking.

In positive education we distinguish between different psychosocial standards we call *actual capacities*. We can divide them into emotionally oriented *primary* and achievement oriented *secondary capacities*. The primary capacities are e.g. *love*, *patience*, *time*, *role-model*, *trust*, *contact*, *sexuality*, *faith* and *unity*. Secondary capacities are e.g. *punctuality*, *orderliness*, *cleanliness*, *obedience*, *courtesy*, *honesty*, *faithfulness*, *justice*, *thrift*, *diligence*, *reliability* and *precision*. These capacities are formed according to the unique developmental conditions of each child during the course of its growing up and socialization. They are absorbed through the capacities to know and to love as mentioned earlier. Every human being owns a complete individually-formed set of actual capacities. These can be useful for society and can serve mankind. Therefore we should try to find a suitable place for everyone in our society with his or her differently-shaped capacity profiles.

When different populations are mixed through migration or other circumstances, it will become necessary for all concerned to be understanding and flexible in order to allow a productive and rewarding cohabitation. In integrating the new arrivals we can learn about each other's strengths and weaknesses and create a new cultural experience in which everyone takes an interest in the other person. The diversity of mankind is of great importance for the development of our society and offers new opportunities for development on a daily basis.

This is why it is so important to provide our little kite flyers with a good set of capacities and rules which they know how to use and can orient themselves by and also to encourage them in their capacity to know and love. We should always keep in mind that ideas of behavior can be very different in other cultures and we therefore have to teach our children to be understanding and respectful of other people's capacities. Furthermore, we can remind ourselves that no system of values is set in stone but is constantly in development depending on sociocultural circumstances.

The Parrot and the sugar sack

A merchant had acquired a very beautiful parrot in India. He loved the bird and spent all his free time with it. Sometimes he would put the parrot on his shoulder, sometimes on his head, and he would always reward it with a piece of sugar. For the parrot, the sugar became the embodiment of his masters love. One evening, the merchant and his parrot were alone in the house. The merchant said, "My dear, it's late and I'm tired. Since tonight there's nobody in the house but us, it's not advisable for both of us to sleep. We have no security here, so watch the house, as though you were a watchman."

The parrot was all ears and set about his task wholeheartedly. Soon the merchant fell into a deep sleep, and the house was enwrapped in a profound silence. Suddenly, a grappling iron was thrown over the wall, and an intruder climbed stealthily up a rope. He tiptoed into the house. Everything he saw he packed into sacks and bags, except for the sugar sack, which he didn't see. Finally there remained nothing but the empty house with the feathered sentinel (who had attentively observed the proceedings), the sugar sack, and the sleeping merchant.

The next morning, when the merchant awoke, he saw gaping emptiness all around him. There was no carpet left to cover the floor or the walls. In vain he searched the empty rooms. "All my fortune and positions have disappeared like smoke in the wind. The house is as empty as the palm in my hand. Where are the silken rugs?" groaned the merchant. "Don't worry," answered the parrot, „the sugar sack is still there." "Where are the jewels?" "Keep your shirt on, the sugar sack is still there." Where are the valuables which brought joy to my soul?" "Be quiet, the sugar sack is still there." "Who was in our house last night?" asked the merchant perplexedly. "A man came, but he didn't stay very long, then he went on his way again," answered the parrot. "Believe me," he swore, "not one sugar cube is missing. Everything you told me, I took to heart. All night long I didn't take my eyes off the sugar sack. You know the sugar is the most valuable thing for us, my lord: How am I supposed to know what's valuable for you?"

(from: Positive Psychotherapy, after P. Etessami, Persian poetess)

In a case of greater difficulties with children, family members or other fellow human beings we can use the established 5-step method for conflict-resolution of Positive Psychotherapy: In the first step – *observation* – we observe the problem and first listen with empathy without offering any personal emotional commentary or attempting an explanation so as not to flare tempers any more than they may already be. The other person first needs to feel understood in their anger and hurt before it is possible for them to open their ears to the concerns of their opposite. Afterwards, we try to resolve the situation constructively and perceptively. In doing so, we manage to interrupt the cycle of reciprocal injuries but not by ignoring the points of conflict. On the contrary, we go one step further and even keep a record of them, point for point, according to facts and circumstances. In the case that other conflict situations arise, we act similarly.

For the next step - *taking inventory* - we take some time to visualize not only the critical but also the positive aspects and qualities of our child or partner. We should do this in writing as well. This way we can work to prevent broad statements and neuroticization arising as a result of a narrowing of perspective.

In the third step - *situational encouragement* - we try to strengthen or, if has collapsed, to rebuild the relationship of trust because we cannot reach a person who closes his mind to us. We have to make an effort to open his mind for us again, i.e. we can value and praise him for his positive qualities and thus strengthen the capacities we admire or find pleasant in him. Like everywhere in life patience is the deciding factor in conflict management.

The joy created in the process leads to more openness which we can use in the fourth step - *verbalization*. Here we use a quiet moment to communicate with our partner or child first the positive events and then the critical events, if possible in a solution-oriented manner. In doing so, we can effect a change of behavior on both sides derived from insight and affection.

In the fifth step – *broadening of goals* – we communicate the new goals we want to achieve together. This creates the energy to carry us into a common future, to inspire us to undertake new projects and to grow together.

As a general recommendation you should have regular family meetings (maybe once a week) where every family member can state a concern in a regularly alternating sequence. It is important not to use hurtful language and to be careful how we treat each other and how we respond, remembering that each person is granted the same amount of time and attention to voice his or her needs and ideas. It is practical to set a time limit and to hold these meetings regularly. It can help to appoint someone different at each meeting to be in charge of time and to moderate the discussion. We have to keep in mind that *no two minds think alike*, that conflict is *normal* and, if resolved constructively, a useful and *creative* part of our daily life. Every person including our children has different values and ideas for the future or is in the process of developing.

"God respects me when I work
but he loves me when I sing."

Rabindranath Tagore

Tips for positive conflict management

Y You and your children are not only victims of circumstance but also unconscious contributors. It is worth investigating this more closely and developing an awareness of it. It is completely acceptable to feel angry, outraged, hurt and/or disappointed at/by the others.

*Do not become a different or better person, but try to accept yourself wholly the way you are now.

*In contrast to actions judged by ethics there are no *good* or *bad* feelings.

*You cannot change the others or your child, you can only change yourself. The other will always be different. Accept this concept and try to get closer.

*State clearly what you want. Your wish is information for your child, not an order.

*It is not enough to tell your child you understand; show it what exactly you have understood.

*You can only reach your child when it listens to you from within. It can only do that when it really feels that you understand.

*Fights, conflicts and aggressions do not have to be harmful to a relationship, quite the contrary, they complete the necessary movement towards harmony.

*It is completely fine to have weaknesses, to show them and to need help with them.

*Harmony, faithfulness, trust and a lively togetherness are not going to fall from the sky, they have to be learned.

*Take the relationship work in your family just as seriously as your professional work.

*Note these three "magic questions":
Do I have to say it? Do I have to say it now? How do I want to say it?

Chapter 7

Out into the big wide world

Many years passed, and then one day it was time for Peppino to finish his A levels. The last year of school had been particularly exhausting and he had been busy studying and practicing. His parents were facing the finals with confidence because their son had learned a lot over the years and gained a lot of flying experience as well. They were rather wondering how high his mark would be, not if he were to pass in general. That really would be a stroke of bad luck should he not pass the exams. Only if his mind went completely blank or if he had an especially mean examiner might his exam be in danger.

When he finally graduated with honors and walked through the school gate for the last time he felt so relieved, as if a big weight was lifted off his shoulders. "Hooray!" he shouted from the top of his lungs. He felt so happy and free! In the evening there was a huge celebration for all the graduates. Peppino had lots of fun with his schoolmates, his teachers, parents and friends. The next morning the big wide world would be waiting for him and, as was customary, the graduates were going "on the wing". This meant traveling around for a year, surviving adventures in the far corners of the world and living on the donations of friendly people along the way.

Peppino wanted to take his trip together with Rebecca and was really looking forward to all the new impressions awaiting them in faraway places. But he was also sorry to have to leave his parents at home. They had spent so many years together, and now, all of a sudden, he was supposed to leave them behind? He was sure to get homesick very soon and to miss them terribly. That scared him a little. He would definitely write to his parents regularly, no question about it. They would also send messages to different post offices along the way. Nevertheless, he and Rebecca would be completely on their own on this great journey, and they would not be able to call for help easily.

The celebration was a real hit. All the invited guests had shown up and the graduates had brought their kites with them. At midnight they rose in the air together for the last time, all of them carrying torches under the full moon. Ardently they showed their parents all of their skills. As if intoxicated they zoomed around, joking and calling out to each other through the balmy night air. When the celebration came to an end in the early hours of the morning and only a few guest remained sitting at the dying out fires, Peppino and Rebecca went home as well. Their parents had left earlier, leaving the two to look into the embers and tell each other stories about the pranks of the past. Only when they got cold and began to shiver did they decide to leave. Peppino took her to her sleeping parents' doorstep and then quickly ran to his own home across the fields and crawled into bed. Tired and happy, he fell asleep immediately.

He dreamed about kite-flying again. It was a wonderful morning and an exquisite rainbow was shimmering in the distance. It must have been raining earlier on, for the world below looked so fresh and green, as if just generously sprinkled by an invigorating spring rain. Once he had heard that there was supposed to be a pot of gold at the end of every rainbow, so he started to move towards the place where the tail of color left the clouds to touch the ground. He got closer and closer to the clouds on the horizon but the end of the rainbow stayed hidden in the distance. Only the rainbow itself became bigger and even more magnificent. The more effort Peppino put into reaching its end, the more unlikely it seemed. Suddenly, when he had almost exhausted all his powers, he saw a glorious golden dragon flying towards him, its body covered in glistening scales and with a head so mighty it seemed to Peppino to have come out of a fairy tale.

At first he was scared. He could not be sure in what mood and to what purpose this amazing magical creature wanted to meet him. The next moment he spotted a tiny rider perched on the creature's shoulders. As they came closer, he was able to recognize the old master his father had told him about so many times. Although he had never seen him in person, the vivid descriptions of his father and Peppino's own gut feeling told him he was right. The dragon rider pulled the rare creature around in a breathtaking curve to sidle up next to Peppino's kite laughing and said: "Dreams are there to fly on, not to be rushed. They inspire our lives while speeding ahead. Some of them you can actually catch, especially the smaller ones.

The tricky thing about dreams is, once you have them in your grasp they start to dissolve. This is why we do not value dreams by how easily we can reach them but rather by the inspiration they bring us. The especially big and beautiful dreams originating from our fantasy can delight us a whole life long, and they change shape and beauty with every obstacle we have successfully overcome along the way. The enthusiasm and awe they can evoke in us when they stay with us for life outweigh by far the short bubbling up of joy when we grasp the dream, which already loses meaning after a few moments and vanishes into thin air.

It is best to carry your dreams in your heart and let them grow and become strong. They will stay with you all your life and will arouse your passions again and again. Also remember that there is no straight road to the fulfillment of your dreams but that the road will reveal itself to you as you move ahead, step by step. Sometimes you will have to take a detour to reach you goal. Do not be disappointed when a dream seems to get away from you. Look back on the wonderful road you will have taken so far. Look back on the astonishing obstacles you overcame. Remember the moving encounters you had and all the amazing experiences your road will have been full of. Sometimes, as you walk your path, your dreams will change and point to new horizons. Above all, however, it is important that you keep your dreams and never lose them. They are an important source of energy and power for you on your way."

With this last sentence, the treasure at the end of the rainbow suddenly lit up and the grandmaster vanished in a cloud of scintillating gold dust. When Peppino tried to grab the pot of gold and pull it into the day, he suddenly woke up. A ray of sunshine had crept through the half-shuttered window and was shining into his face. He caught the smell of coffee and hot chocolate and he knew that his mother, for the last time before his great journey, had made him breakfast. The family sat down together, and over a cup of hot chocolate and a bread roll with jam Peppino told his parents about his strange dream. Volavento reflected thoughtfully for a moment on the wise man's words and then said: "Peppino, I think it's time you interpreted your dreams yourself. Maybe, somewhere along your travels, you will meet the old man and he will tell you about his great dreams."

Together on the doorstep, Volavento and Regina said goodbye to their son with a hearty hug, cautioned and blessed him with many fond words and asked him to stay safe. With mixed feelings they watched as he flew to Rebecca's house. A short time later two young kite flyers rose waving into the deep blue sky towards the mountains on the horizon.

Perhaps you have heard if these two found the old man on their journeys in the world? And if they've not grown tired yet, they're flying to this day.

To say goodbye, or: When it is hard to let go

When we are talking about saying goodbye to our grown up kite flyers, it is important to be able to say with conviction that we gave them our *best* parenting, infinite love, ample time and a big treasure of experiences. If we honestly feel we did that, then we do not have to worry about their well-being. They will not know how to react in every situation of course, but they will have the tools to accept every challenge. We can release them into freedom with a good conscience without having to spend sleepless nights.

When the time has come, we must be able to detach ourselves from our children, release them from the nourishing but also constricting umbilical cord of family life and set them free. Just as we experience different phases in every encounter, hearty greetings and attachment, conflict and differentiation and the goodbyes and detachments, so, too, do we see these same processes at work in the development of a child: Attachment with a lot of warmth at birth and in the first years, then differentiation during childhood and puberty, then a farewell after the successful integration of capacities during puberty and adolescence. We can say with certainty that this goodbye will only be temporary and our children will always find their way back home. Our relationship simply moves to a different level and we can continue to enjoy our lives together.

To secure the successful detachment of our young kite flyers we as well have to make great changes in our lives to overcome the grief of the loss of our children and supplant it with a joy in our hearts for having found dear friends who will also always stay our children. The room they have taken up in our lives will get smaller and smaller during the course of their development. We cannot ask them to continue to fill it. When we look at the four modes of our lives we will notice that the time and emotion we invest in our social environment and partly into the work raising our children is reduced, and a *hole* or *vacuum* opens up. This hole can also have a psychosomatic effect which can be quite unpleasant. It will be necessary to compensate this loss, in other words, fill the now freed up space with other activities like friendships, hobbies and other meaningful things and pleasures we've always wanted or could rediscover. This is not about covering up an ugly hole, it is more about entering a new stage in life, to fill it with new purpose and to give the young adult the earned and needed freedom. When our children spread their (kite) wings, a meaningful part of our life is missing, that daily 'being there' for our children. That is why we are called upon to look for and find new meaning in life. This demand cannot be placed onto our children anymore and it is important for them that they are set free from it completely.

When the children are out of the house, have finished their education and start their own families, we can again be part of the miracle of children growing up and we can take over some of the tasks burdening the young parents. This can be a great joy if we don’t make the mistake of claiming the role of the parents and trespassing on our children's terrain. When we act appropriately, we will be able to place at their disposal our significant treasure of experiences. The parents of our grandchildren will always be our children. This is something we should always know is true.

A rooftop garden

One summer night, the members of a family slept in the garden on top of their house. To her great displeasure, the mother saw that her son and his

One summer night, the members of a family slept in the garden on top of their house. To her great displeasure, the mother saw that her son and his wife (whom she barely tolerated anyway) were snuggled up against each other. Unable to bear this sight, she woke them both up and cried, "How can you sleep so close together in this heat? It's unhealthy and dangerous." In another corner of the garden, there slept her daughter and son-in-law, whom she adored. They were sleeping apart from each other, with at least a foot of space between them. The mother woke them up gently by saying, "My darlings, how can you sleep so far apart when it's as chilly as this? Why don't you warm each other up?" The daughter-in-law heard this. She sat up and, with a loud voice, uttered the following words like a prayer: "How mighty is our God. A rooftop garden and such a variable climate."

(The Merchant and the parrot)

"A happy mother
is a greater blessing for her children
than a hundred guidebooks on parenting."

Heinrich Pestalozzi

Tips for detachment

When it is time for farewell you can rest assured that you have provided a good upbringing with love, time and experience.

*Be happy about the road you travelled together with your children.

*Concentrate on your new stage of life, and discover new possibilities for development.

*Use your new freedom, and strive for real meaning in life.

*Take an interest in the further plans and fantasies of your children. Be happy with them.

*You have the possibility to experience new family life with your children and to accompany them in their new stage of life in an appropriate role.

Epilogue

This book is now at an end. All that remains is to wish you lots of fun *playing* with your children and young people. Very few things allow the lightness of being and the source of curiosity and youth to shine forth in the way that *playing* does. Every day you can find new, fresh experiences with your little artists and be amazed at how the world inspires them and how they greet it with open arms.

Although there will be difficult times in your life and in the lives of your children, you will, nonetheless, know with certainty that every dark night ends in the light of day and that you will progress a little bit further every day in your development. Every difficulty is a challenge to be overcome. Your aim, together with your little adventurers, is to achieve new strengths. Conflicts enable you and others to get to know yourselves better. Sad moments can be as helpful as times of pausing to reflect and take stock of what is around you. At any time, you can discover the true simplicity and beauty of all things with the open eyes of your children.

The world is full of wonders. Keep in mind that everything that exists is a product of a single Big Bang which produced such diversity that you may ask yourself the question: "What wonders does the future hold in store for human beings and all the living creatures of this world to touch our souls?"

In Memory of Nossrat Peseschkian

Youth is not a stage of life. It is a state of mind, a mood of your will, the nature of ideas, the vitality of your emotions, the dominance of courage over anxiety and the desire for adventure over the tendency for laziness. Nobody ages just by the passing of years alone. We only grow older when we give up our ideals. Age creases the skin, but if you give up your enthusiasm, your soul becomes creased. Discontentment and doubt, mistrusting oneself, fear and despair bows the head and makes the striving spirit descend into dust. Whether seventy or seventeen, in every beating heart lives the love of wonder, the delighted amazement at the stars and star-like things and thoughts and at the fearless encounter with events. There lives the insatiable and childlike yearning for the next new thing, for joy and the dance of life.

You are

as young as your faith and as old as your doubt,

as young as your self-confidence and as old as your fear,

as young as your hope and as old as your despair.

Marcus Aurelius

If your senses and your instincts lay down-trodden, the center of your heart is blanketed with the snow of pessimism and the ice of cynicism, then yes, you have truly grown old and may God have mercy on your soul. Yet as long as your heart can receive the tidings of beauty, joy, courage, greatness and power which emanate from the earth, its people and from the Eternal, you will stay young.

(The Naked Emperor)

Acknowledgements

I am delighted to dedicate this book to my parents Margarete and Jürgen. They have given me, from my childhood onwards, the love, the role model and the fundamental life experiences which have been necessary for writing this book. I would also like to thank my siblings Gunver and Stephan for our shared childhood and youth and the lessons of love and tolerance learnt. It gives me pleasure to say that I am thoroughly happy with everything that we experienced as a family.

I would also like to mention Erika and Ernst Zölß who have always been like second parents to me.

Warmest gratitude is owed to Professor Nossrat Peseschkian and Dr Nawid Peseschkian for the joyful and inspirational collaboration on this book, as well as for being like a father and brother in all those years when we worked together.

Just as important to me were the caring mentorship of Manije Peseschkian that went beyond the training required for psychotherapy, as well as the knowledge conveyed and the living example of the positive conception of man provided by Dr Gunther Hübner, John Okoro, Dr Hamid

Peseschkian, Arno Remmers, Sheyda Rafat, Birgit Werner, Dr Wolfgang Hönmann and all the other lecturers of the WIAP.

Maike Löffelhardt-Michel has brought our book to life with her dreamlike drawings. The days that we spent laughing and being creative in the cafe did my soul a world of good. I had been looking for an illustrator who could draw such pictures for a very, very long time before I found her through a wonderful twist of fate.

I thank Sarah Luscher and her parents, Albrecht and Christel Luscher, for their active support in the handling of the written text, the corrections and the inspiration for change. I am intimately indebted to Elena Bellavia because through her and through fate Professor Nossrat Peseschkian found his way into my life.

I am also deeply indebted to Libertad Ordoñez, whose loving support gave me the necessary drive to take the last steps to publishing this book. Many thanks to my editor Ina Kleinod, who inspired me and contributed considerably to the beauty of this book.

And thus the wondrous cooperation of many people orchestrated the full radiance of this book. May it shine into many hearts.

References

Peseschkian, Nossrat:

Positive Psychotherapie. © S. Fischer Verlag GmbH, Frankfurt am Main 1977

Psychotherapie des Alltagslebens. © S. Fischer Verlage, Frankfurt am Main 1977

Der Kaufmann und der Papagei. © Fischer Taschenbuch Verlag GmbH, Frankfurt am Main 1979

Positive Familientherapie. © S. Fischer Verlage, Frankfurt am Main 1982

Auf der Suche nach Sinn. © S. Fischer Verlage, Frankfurt am Main 1983

33 und eine Form der Partnerschaft. © S. Fischer Verlage, Frankfurt am Main 1988

Psychosomatik und Positive Psychotherapie. © S. Fischer Verlage, Frankfurt am Main 1993

Das Geheimnis des Samenkorns. © S. Fischer Verlage, Frankfurt am Main 1996

Der nackte Kaiser. © 1997 Pattloch Verlag GmbH & Co. KG, München

Es ist leicht, das Leben schwer zu nehmen, aber schwer, das Leben leicht zu nehmen. © Herder Verlag, Freiburg 2006

Wenn du etwas haben willst, was du noch nie gehabt hast, dann musst du etwas tun, was du noch nie getan hast. © Herder Verlag, Freiburg 2007

Glaube an Gott und binde dein Kamel fest. © Kreuz Verlag, Stuttgart 2008

Boessmann, Udo/Peseschkian, Nossrat.: Positive Ordnungstherapie. © Hippocrates Verlag, Stuttgart 1995

Peseschkian, Nossrat/Battegay Raymond : Die Treppe zum Glück. © S. Fischer Verlage, Frankfurt am Main 2006

Peseschkian, Nossrat/Anas Aziz: Lexikon der Positiven Psychotherapie. © S. Fischer Verlage, Frankfurt am Main 2009

Peseschkian, Nossrat/Nawid Peseschkian/Hamid Pesesch- kian: Wenn du etwas haben willst, was du noch nie gehabt hast, dann musst du etwas tun, was du noch nie getan hast. © Trias Verlag, Stuttgart 2009

Peseschkian, Nossrat/Christian Clever: Goldene Regeln der Lebenskunst. © Herder Verlag, Freiburg 2012

Kahlil Gibran: Der Prophet. Aus dem Englischen von Giovanni und Ditte Bandini. © der deutschsprachigen Übersetzung: 2002 Deutscher Taschenbuch Verlag München

Stephan Schuhmacher (Hrsg.): Chinesische Weisheiten. © 2004 Deutscher Taschenbuch Verlag, München.

Antonovsky, Aaron: Salutogenese. © DGVT, Tübingen 1997

Zeitfracht Medien GmbH
Ferdinand-Jühlke-Straße 7
99095 Erfurt, Deutschland
produktsicherheit@kolibri360.de